Nita Mehta®

C000179803

Art of
BAKING
EGGLESS

Nita Mehta®
B.Sc. (Home Science)
M.Sc. (Food and Nutrition) Gold Medalist

Nita Mehta®
Art of
BAKING
EGGLESS

SNAB
Excellence in Books

Snab Publishers Pvt Ltd
3A/3, Asaf Ali Road, New Delhi 110 002

Recipe Development & Testing:
Nita Mehta Foods - R & D Centre
3A/3, Asaf Ali Road, New Delhi - 110002

Nita Mehta
CREATIVE ARTS
Creating Food Artists, not just chefs...

© Copyright Snab Publishers Pvt Ltd 2015

All rights reserved

ISBN 978-81-7869-495-5

First Print 2015

Printed in India at Nova Publications & Printers Pvt. Ltd.

Contributing Writers :
Anurag Mehta
Tanya Mehta
Subhash Mehta

Editors :
Sangeeta
Sunita

Distributed by :
NITA MEHTA BOOKS
3A/3, Asaf Ali Road, New Delhi - 02

Distribution Centre :
D16/1, Okhla Industrial Area, Phase-I,
New Delhi - 110020
Tel.: 26813199, 26813200
E-mail: nitamehta.mehta@gmail.com
Website: www.nitamehta.com

Editorial and Marketing office
E-159, Greater Kailash II, New Delhi 110 048

Food Styling and Photography by Snab
Typesetting by National Information Technology Academy
3A/3, Asaf Ali Road, New Delhi 110 002

Nita Mehta
Books
Distributors & Publishers

Let your Traditional Home *Recipes* become your Identity!

All homes have one or more unique recipes which is passed down from generations to generations. At Rasoishop, we are collecting such unique traditional recipes (Vegetarian) for publishing in our book. If you have an original mouth watering traditional recipe, send it to us alongwith the image of the recipe and a brief about you!

Whats more? You get to feature in Rasoishop CookBook and the Best recipe in each category will be awarded ₹ 11,000 / -cash prize!

Category :

1. Breakfast

2. Main course

3. Rice

4. Dessert

5. Pickle & Chutney etc.

Send your recipe through email: recipes@rasoishop.com

Unique Recipe **Terms & Conditions:**
- Only vegetarian dishes are allowed
- All recipe rights will be reserved by rasoishop.com

- Every decision of rasoishop management will be final and binding
- Correspondence or debate will not be entertained
- Subject to Gandhidham Jurisdiction

Shop Online : www.rasoishop.com

"A party without cake is really just a meeting"- Julia Child

Congratulations on your purchase of Bakeware set from Rasoishop.com! Counting you among our customers is something for which we are especially grateful.

You are only 1 step away from experiencing the joy of baking. This bakeware set alongwith the recipe book is designed to be an experience - the delight of baking desserts at home, the fresh aroma, watching the cake rise in the oven and the butter-cream frosting thickening up to the right consistency - and having achieved all this - to see your child take the first bite full of love and cream and cake, you know that today you have baked!

We hope you truly enjoy and engage in this experience. Rasoishop.com has tied up exclusively with Mrs. Nita Mehta to present to you her baking recipes and techniques. This book will guide you step by step and also demonstrate techniques and tips for amateur cooks!

Happy Baking and Happy Shopping!

Team Rasoishop

Introduction

No birthday or anniversary is complete without that special cake, which is made with a lot of love and good wishes. This book will give you the confidence to make cakes, which are simple to make yet beautiful to look at and of course delicious to eat. Treat your guests with pies, tarts & pastries after a meal and get rewarded by their compliments. Tea time cakes will fill your home with the baking aroma, bringing happiness and joy to family & friends.

Chocolate! The mere mention of anything associated with this mouth watering confection can cause a dreamy look to come into the eyes of the chocoholic. You can make a variety of flavours & gift it to your loved ones.

A few baked savoury dishes are included which will complete the book.

Happy Baking!

Nita Mehta

Contents

Handy Tips

- All ingredients should be at room temperature for best results.
- Check expiry dates of ingredients, especially essences, baking powder and baking soda before use.
- Sift dry ingredients well, so that the mixture is aerated.
- Use the correct size cake moulds.
- A prepared cake mixture should go straight into the hot oven.
- Always bake in the centre of the oven.
- Beating butter and sugar together is important. This is called creaming. The mixture should be beaten so well that it starts looking like whipped cream and becomes really fluffy and light.

- Add essence to the fat because fat absorbs flavour readily.
- Sometimes the cake batter may appear too thick even though you may have measured the ingredients very carefully, as stated in the recipe. This happens because of the grade of flour that has been used. In such cases, you may conveniently add 2-4 tbsp of milk to make the batter softer.
- When the recipe calls for 'beating', use an electric hand mixer to beat the mixture till light and fluffy. If the recipe says to 'mix well', just mix all ingredients with a spatula till well combined. Do not overmix or overbeat.
- Do not beat the batter after the flour has been added or the finished cake will turn out heavy. Simply use a spatula to fold the flour in.
- Fill cake moulds only two-thirds full of batter, leaving enough space for it to rise.
- Tap filled cake moulds gently on the kitchen platform to release any large air bubbles.
- For even distribution of fruit and to avoid sinking of the dried fruit, mix fruit with a little flour before adding to the cake mixture.
- For party cakes, brush sugar syrup on cakes with a silicon brush.
- When cakes are removed from the oven, wait for 10-15 minutes before removing from the mould. Always remove cakes on a wire rack.
- A microwave oven on microwave mode cannot be used for baking any contents of this book. Only the convection mode of the microwave oven can be used for baking.

Problems with the Cake...

QUALITY OF CAKE	REASONS - ANY ONE OR MORE
Heavy Cake	Too little baking powder. Too much flour. Mixture (butter and sugar) not creamed enough. Flour mixed in too vigorously. Oven too slow (cake takes too long to get done).
A Dry Cake	Too much baking powder or flour. Not enough fat or liquid. Too long in the oven.
A Sunken Cake	Too much liquid. Too much baking powder or sugar. Too little flour. Oven door slammed or cake moved during baking. Taken out from the oven too soon.
A Peaked Cake	Insufficient butter/oil or baking powder/soda. Too much flour. Oven temperature too high.
A Badly Cracked Top	Oven too hot. Cake tin too small. Too much flour. Not enough liquid.
Fruit Sunk to the Bottom	Fruit not properly dried and then coated with flour. Cake mixture too thin. Fruit added before adding the flour.

Tea Time Cakes

Basic Vanilla Cake

Makes: ½ kg

INGREDIENTS

½ tin condensed milk (200 gm)
3 tbsp powdered sugar
½ cup oil
1 cup flour (*maida*)
¼ cup cornflour
½ tsp baking soda (*mitha soda*)
1 tsp baking powder
½ cup milk, approx.
1 tsp vanilla essence
¼ cup soda water (a bottle of soda)

1. Sift flour with cornflour, baking soda and baking powder. Keep aside.
2. Mix sugar and condensed milk. Beat till light. Add oil. Beat well to mix.
3. Add half of the flour and half the milk. Mix well with a silicon spatula. Add essence. Add the remaining flour and the milk mixing well after the addition. Pour soda water and mix quickly.
4. Immediately pour batter in the big square silicon mould. Bake for 45 minutes in a preheated oven at 150°C/300°F.

Sugar Free Vanilla Cake

Makes: 250 gm

INGREDIENTS

3/4 cup yogurt
1 tbsp lemon juice
45 gms salted butter (1/4 cup)
1/3 cup + 1 tbsp sugar free powder
100 gms flour (*maida*)
1 tsp baking powder
1 tsp baking soda (*mitha soda*)
2-3 tbsp milk

1. Sieve flour, baking powder and baking soda together. keep aside
2. Beat sugar free powder and butter very well. Add honey.
3. In a separate bowl, mix yogurt and lemon juice.
4. To the beaten sugar free powder and butter, fold in sieved flour alternately with yogurt and lemon juice mixture with a spatula. Do not over mix.
5. Add milk and mix gently. Put immediately in the big square silicon mould. Bake in the preheated oven at 180°C/350°F for 30 minutes or till the cake is done.

Sugar Free Chocolate Cake

For sugar free chocolate cake, use 80 gm flour and 20 gm cocoa powder instead of 100 gm flour in the above recipe.

Chocolate Cake

Serves 10

INGREDIENTS

2½ cups flour (*maida*)
½ cup cocoa powder
1½ tsp baking powder
1½ cup sugar
¾ cup butter - softened
1 cup curd - use fresh curd
1 tsp vanilla *essence*
½ cup milk
3 tbsp mix fruit jam

1. Sift flour, cocoa and baking powder together. Keep aside.

2. Beat sugar and butter till light and fluffy.

3. Add curd, vanilla essence and jam to it and mix well.

4. Fold in flour with a silicon spatula. Add enough milk to get a soft batter.

5. Transfer mixture to the big square silicon mould. Level it.

6. Bake in a preheated oven at 180°C/350°F for 30 minutes. Remove from oven after 5 minutes.

Carrot Cinnamon Cake

Serves 8

INGREDIENTS

100 gms butter
100 gms castor sugar
1 cup milk
1 tsp vanilla essence
1 tsp cinnamon (dalchini) powder
200 gms flour (*maida*)
1 tsp baking powder
½ tsp baking soda
50 gms walnuts - finely chopped
175 gms carrots (2 carrots) - peeled & grated
a drop of orange food colour, optional

1. Sieve flour with baking powder and baking soda.

2. Cream the butter and sugar in a bowl until light and fluffy. Add essence and beat again.

3. And 1-2 tbsp of flour and half of milk. Mix well with a spatula. Add the remaining milk and fold in the remaining flour.

4. Add the cinnamon powder and grated carrots to the batter and fold gently. Add colour if needed.

5. Pour into the big square silicon mould, sprinkle walnuts and bake at 180°C/350°F for 35 minutes.

Lemon Yogurt Cake

Serves 10

1. For the rind, peel one firm lemon as thinly as possible with a sharp knife, peeling only the upper yellow skin & leaving the white pith beneath. Shred the peel into very thin ½" long strips.

2. Sieve flour, baking powder and baking soda together. Keep aside.

3. Beat sugar and butter very well. Mix lemon peel.

4. Separately mix yogurt and lemon juice in a bowl and keep aside.

5. To the beaten sugar and butter, fold in sieved flour alternately with yogurt and lemon juice mixture with a silicon spatula. Add milk and mix gently.

6. Put immediately in the big square silicon mould. Bake in the preheated oven at 375°F/190°C for 30 min or till done.

7. The cake is very soft, so let it cool in the mould for 10 minutes and then remove to a wire rack.

8. For the topping, heat sugar, lemon rind and lemon juice over low heat, stirring continuously, till the sugar dissolves. Add a drop of yellow colour.

9. Pierce top of the cake with a fork and pour the prepared topping on top of the cake. Cool the cake uncovered, at least for 2 hours before cutting.

Date and Walnut Cake

Serves 8

INGREDIENTS

½ tin condensed milk (200 gm)
½ cup (60 gm) oil
250 gm dates
1 cup less 1 tbsp (85 gm) flour (*maida*)
½ cup walnuts - chopped finely
½ tsp vanilla essence
1 tsp baking powder
½ tsp baking soda (*mitha so*da)

1. Remove seeds from dates and chop them finely. Add 6 tbsp of water and keep on low flame for 2 minutes. Remove from fire. Add ½ tsp baking soda. Keep aside for 15-20 minutes.

2. Sift flour with baking powder. Mix dates and walnuts with flour.

3. Beat oil and condensed milk very well. Add essence. Mix. Add flour. Beat well. Bake in a preheated oven at 150°C/300°F for 40 minutes, or till done.

Honey Ginger Victorian Cake

Serves 8

INGREDIENTS

150 gm (1½ cups) flour (*maida*)
85 gm (slightly less than ¾ cup) sugar
100 gm (2/3 cup) butter
½ cup milk
3 tbsp honey
2 tsp dry ginger powder
1½ tbsp white vinegar
½ tsp baking powder
½ tsp baking soda

1. Preheat oven to 190°C/375°F.
2. Sift flour. Rub flour and butter together with the finger tips, till the mixture is crumbly. Do not over mix.
3. Add ginger powder, baking powder and sugar and mix lightly.
4. Divide milk into two parts. To one part add vinegar.
5. Warm the other part of milk slightly and add baking soda. Now mix both the milks together with a silicon spatula.
6. The milk will start foaming (bubbles appear). Add this to the cake dough very quickly. Mix fast and well. Add honey and mix.
7. Transfer to a big square silicon mould and bake in preheated oven at 190°C/375°F for 20 minutes, then lower the temperature to 150°C/300°F for another 20 minutes.
8. Let cake cool in the mould for 5 minutes before removing to a wire rack.

Pineapple Upside Down

Serves 12

½ tin (200 gms) condensed milk
140 gms (1¼ cups) flour (*maida*)
1 tsp baking powder
½ tsp baking soda
90 gms (½ cup) butter
4 tbsp powdered sugar
½ cup milk
1½ tsp pineapple essence
a few drops yellow colour, optional
2-3 tbsp brown sugar for caramelisation
4-5 rings (slices) of pineapple - tinned
a few glace cherries - cut into two pieces
a few almonds - soaked & skin removed
(blanched)

5. Add half of flour and half of the milk to the condensed milk mixture. Mix with a silicon spatula. Add the remaining flour and the milk and mix well.

6. Pour into the decorated cake tin, on top of the pineapple rings. Bake in a preheated oven at 150°C/300°F for 30-40 minutes. When the cake is done, remove from oven, loosen sides of the cake and immediately turn onto a wire rack. (Do not cool in the tin).

1. Grease a 7" round cake tin. Sprinkle brown sugar. Arrange a drained pineapple ring in the centre. Arrange halved or full pineapple rings on the sides, with a cherry half in the centre of each ring. Place the cherry with the flat, cut side touching the bottom of the tin. Arrange split almonds in between the rings with the flat side touching the bottom of the tin. Keep tin aside.

2. To prepare the cake, melt butter in a pan. Cool. Add sugar and condensed milk.

3. Beat well. Add colour and essence.

4. Sieve flour, baking powder and baking soda.

Note: This cake can be made the big square silicon mould provided in the bakeware set.

All Time Favourite Chocolate Brownie

Serves 8

INGREDIENTS

1¼ cups milk (skim milk)
2 tbsp white vinegar
1½ cups flour (*maida*)
¼ cup cocoa powder
1 tsp baking soda (*mitha soda*)
1½ cups plus 2 tbsp powdered sugar
½ cup oil, 1 tsp vanilla essence
¼ cup crushed walnuts

TOPPING

40 gm dark cooking chocolate - chopped
3 tbsp icing sugar

1. To make paneer, boil milk. Add vinegar. When the milk starts to curdle, keep on fire for ½ minute. Remove from fire. Let the paneer cool down along with the whey to room temperature. Crumble the paneer gently.

2. Sift flour, baking soda, cocoa powder and sugar and mix well with the spoon. Put all the dry ingredients in the mixing bowl.

3. Add oil and the paneer alongwith the water (whey). Add essence. Mix well with a silicon spatuala.

4. Put in big square silicon mould.

5. Sprinkle walnuts and bake at 160°/325°F for 40 minutes.

6. Remove from oven. Let it cool down completely.

7. For the topping, melt chopped chocolate with 1-2 tbsp water in a heavy bottom pan on very low heat. You can also melt chocolate in a double boiler. If the flame is high, the chocolate will sieze into a hard lump. Remove from fire when chocolate is smooth. Add icing sugar and mix well. Drizzle topping on the brownie. Let it set.

8. Cut into squares to serve.

Healthy Banana Oat Brownie

Serves 8

INGREDIENTS

100 gms flour (*maida*)
¼ cup oats
75 gms cooking chocolate - chopped
1¼ tsp baking powder
½ tsp baking soda (*mitha soda*)
½ cup butter - softened
1 tsp vanilla essence
150 gms caster sugar
2 large ripe bananas - chopped

TOPPING (MIX TOGETHER)
¼ cup oats, 1 tbsp butter melted
2 tbsp brown sugar

1. Sift flour, baking powder and soda.
2. Add oats and keep aside.
3. Microwave butter and chocolate in a microwave for 1 minute. Mix well to melt the chocolate. If need be, microwave for 30 seconds more. Add essence.
4. Mash bananas with a fork in a big bowl. Beat bananas & sugar. Add essence.
5. Add melted chocolate to bananas.
6. Add flour and cocoa mixture and mix with a silicon spatula.
7. Transfer to a big square silicon mould. Sprinkle the topping mixture. Bake for 35-40 minutes at 180°C/350°C in a preheated oven.

Party Cakes
& Pastries

German Blueberry Cake

Serves 16

INGREDIENTS

vanilla cake, as on page 9
1 cup blueberry topping and 2 tsp cornflour,
see tip
50 gms (½ cup) chopped dark chocolate
250 gms (1¼ cups) whipping cream
¼ cup chopped white chocolate for making
nets, (see page 23)
black grapes and strawberries, optional

SUGAR SYRUP

¼ cup sugar boiled with ½ cup water for 2-3
minutes, cool completely

1. For the cake, make batter by following the recipe on page 9. Transfer batter into a big square silicon mould. Bake at 150°C/300°F for 45 minutes. Check with tooth pick.

2. For blueberry topping, mix 2 tsp cornflour in ¼ cup water. Cook till it becomes thick. Remove from fire. Add 2-3 tbsp berry topping and mix gently. Add the remaining blueberry topping and stir gently to mix. You can also make home made topping as given below.

3. Beat cream at medium speed until thick. Put about 1 cup whipped cream in the icing bag. Keep aside.

4. Melt ½ cup dark chocolate for 30 seconds in a microwave or on a double boiler. Keep aside.

5. Cut the cake into 3 layers. Place a layer of the cake on a serving platter. Spread melted chocolate on it with a palette knife. Keep in the fridge for 10 minutes for the chocolate to set.

6. Spread some blueberry topping on the chocolate. Place 2nd layer of cake on it. Soak with ¼ cup sugar syrup. Spread some cream on top. Place the last layer of cake. Soak again. Spread cream on top and sides to cover completely.

7. Make big swirls joining each other on the edges with cream in the bag, forming a border all around. Refrigerate to set.

8. Fill the centre with berry topping. Melt white chocolate for 30 seconds in a microwave. Add 2-3 drops oil and stir to get a flowing consistency. Make nets as given on page 23. Decorate with nets and fresh fruits.

TIP: HOME MADE BERRY TOPPING

Mix ¾ cup black raisins in 1 cup (200 ml) ready made grape juice and keep on fire. Dissolve 3 tsp cornflour in ½ cup water and add to the boiling raisins. Stir on low heat till thick. Add 2-3 tbsp strawberry or mixed fruit jam. Add some raspberry red colour if needed. Cool and use. Omit step 2.

Cappuccino Hazelnut Cake

Serves 14-16

INGREDIENTS

140 gms (1¼ cups) flour (*maida*)
30 gms (½ cup) cocoa powder
1 tsp baking powder
½ tsp baking soda (*mitha soda*)
¾ cup yogurt
150 gms (1¼ cup) powdered sugar
½ cup oil
3 tsp coffee powder mixed in 1 tbsp hot water
1 tsp vanilla essence
3 tbsp milk

COFFEE SYRUP FOR SOAKING
3 tsp coffee powder
¼ cup brown sugar, ½ cup water

COFEE ICING
300 gms whipping cream (Rich's cream)
1-2 tbsp icing sugar, or to taste
3 tsp coffee powder mixed in 3 tbsp hot water

OTHER INGREDIENTS
4 tbsp chocolate hazelnut paste (ready made) -
microwave if hard
1 tbsp cocoa - to sift on top

1. Sift flour, baking powder, baking soda and cocoa powder together.

2. Combine coffee and hot water. Beat yogurt and sugar to mix well. Add coffee mix and essence. Add oil very gradually, while beating continuously.

3. Fold in flour mixture with silicon spatula gently. Add 3 tbsp milk. Mix gently.

4. Transfer mixture into the big square silicon mould. Bake in preheated oven at 160°C /325°F for 40 minutes. After 5 minutes transfer cake to the wire rack.

5. For coffee syrup, boil water and sugar on low heat for 2-3 minutes till sugar melts. Remove from heat. Add coffee.

6. For icing, whip cream till soft peaks form. Keep aside. Add icing sugar and coffee dissolved in water. Fold this into the whipped cream with a spatula.

7. Cut cake into 3 layers. Keep one layer on a serving platter. Soak with 3-4 tbsp of the cooled coffee syrup.

8. Spread some coffee flavoured icing.

9. Put some hazelnut paste on the second layer of cake and invert on the cake spread with icing.

10. Soak cake again and spread icing. Spread hazelnut paste on the last layer and invert on cream icing. Soak again.

11. Spread coffee icing on top & sides. Level with a palette knife dipped in a tall glass of cold water. Refrigerate till chilled.

12. Sift cocoa on the cake through a tea strainer. If you like, put strips of paper on the cake and then sift cocoa powder. Pick up paper gently.

Strawberry Layered Pastry

Serves 10

INGREDIENTS

vanilla cake recipe, page 9
4 tbsp strawberry crush
a few almonds - blanched, peeled & sliced

BUTTER ICING
100 gm unsalted butter, softened
200 gm icing sugar
2 tbsp strawberry crush
1 tsp strawberry essence
1-2 drops strawberry red colour

TOPPING
2 tbsp strawberry crush
1½ tsp cornflour mixed with 2 tbsp water.

1. Prepare a cake batter as given on page 9. To make strawberry cake, add ½ tsp strawberry essence along with vanilla essence, in the recipe.

2. Cool the cake. Slice the cake horizontally into 2 parts.

3. For the butter icing, beat together the butter and icing sugar, until smooth and fluffy. Add crush, essence and just a drop of colour. Add more if needed.

4. Place the first piece of cake on the serving plate. Spread 3-4 tbsp of strawberry icing on it. Spread some almonds. Keep in the fridge for 5-10 minutes so that the icing sets. Keep left over icing also in the fridge.

5. Spread 2 tbsp crush on the second piece of cake & invert carefully on the first piece of cake spread with icing. Press well.

6. Cover top completely with icing. Chill cake in the freezer for 10 minutes. To smoothen the top, put hot water in a glass & dip a long knife in it. Run the knife lightly on the chilled icing to get a smooth top.

7. For topping, put strawberry crush in a small pan. Add cornflour paste and mix well with a silicon spatula. Bring to a boil and simmer on low heat, stirring for 1-2 minutes. Let it col slightly and fill in a paper cone. Draw lines on the cake. Refrigerate till set.

8. Cut into rectangular pieces.

21

Truffle Cake

Serves 10-12

INGREDIENTS

1 chocolate cake, given on page 10
200 gms whipping cream, preferably Rich's

SUGAR SYRUP TO SOAK
1/3 cup sugar and ¾ cup water
1½ tbsp cocoa powder

TRUFFLE ICING
200 gms cream, preferably Amul
225 gm cooking chocolate - chopped (2¼ cups)
1 tsp butter

1. Make a chocolate cake as given on page 10. Make sugar syrup by boiling water and sugar together. After the boil, keep syrup on low heat for 2-3 minutes to get a slightly sticky syrup. Add cocoa powder. Remove from heat and cool completely. Keep in the fridge.

2. To make truffle icing, heat 200 gms cream in a heavy bottom pan on low heat till it becomes hot. Do not let it boil. Add 225 gms chocolate to it. Mix nicely with a silicon spatula to remove any lumps. Remove from fire when almost melted and mix well with a silicon spatula. Add butter. Keep aside.

3. Beat 200 gms whipping cream till stiff peaks form.

4. Mix about ½ cup truffle at room temperature, from step 2, to the whipped cream to get a light brown chocolate cream. Keep chocolate cream in the fridge. Keep remaining truffle aside for top coating, outside the fridge, so that the chocolate remains melted.

5. Cut chocolate cake into 3 layers.

6. Put a layer of cake on a plate, soak lightly with syrup. Spread ¼ of the prepared chocolate cream on it. Place the second layer of cake on it. Soak with 1/3 cup of syrup, using a brush. Spread some chocolate cream on it. Place the top layer of cake on it. Again soak with 1/3 cup syrup.

7. Trim the sides. Cover the top and sides of the cake with the remaining chocolate cream. Keep it in the freezer for 15-20 minutes, till cream becomes firm.

8. Keep cake on a rack. Place a plate under the rack. Check truffle. The truffle can be reheated with 1-2 tbsp water, if it has become too thick. It should be thin enough to flow properly.

9. Pour the prepared truffle on the set cake and tilt rack to cover the sides of the cake also.

10. Decorate cake with curved sticks and nets as given on the next page.

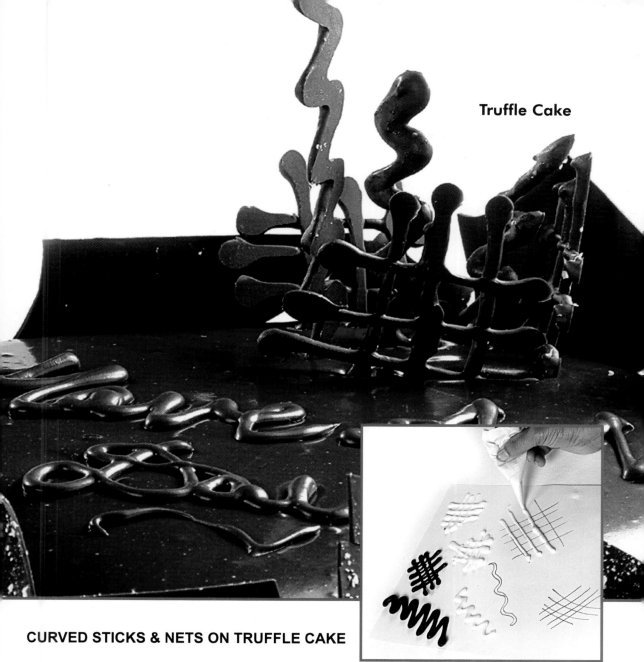

Truffle Cake

CURVED STICKS & NETS ON TRUFFLE CAKE

Chocolate Nets

For nets, draw crisscross lines on any paper. Make a cone with butter paper. Secure cone with scotch tape. Put melted white chocolate or dark chocolate in the cone. Cut out a slightly big tip. Pipe chocolate on the drawn lines on the paper. Freeze paper for 5 minutes. Peel off the paper carefully to take out nets from paper. Keep nets for atleast 1 hour in the freezer on a plate to become hard and firm. Arrange on cakes and desserts.

Chocolate Curved Sticks

Fill melted chocolate in a paper cone. Cut out a slightly big tip. Squeeze out tall zig-zag lines on paper. Freeze paper and peel off as above.

Butter-Scotch Fresh Fruit Gateau

Serves 8

INGREDIENTS

a vanilla cake, page 9
250 gm whipping cream
6 tbsp icing sugar
1 tsp butter scotch essence
2-3 tbsp strawberry jam or crush
½ cup orange juice, ready made

TOPPING
different coloured fresh fruits - strawberries,
apple, kiwi, grapes, cherries, orange

GLAZE SYRUP
¼ cup sugar, ¼ cup water
½ tsp butter

CARAMEL SUGAR
½ cup sugar
20 almonds - chopped

1. Prepare a vanilla cake as given on page 9, in a big square silicon mould.

2. Whip cream with essence and powdered sugar till firm peaks are formed. Put some cream in an icing bag. Refrigerate the remaining cream and the bag.

3. For caramel sugar, put sugar in a non stick pan. Spread out in a flat layer covering the bottom of the pan. Keep on medium heat for 2-3 minutes without touching the sugar. When the sugar starts to turn light golden, remove from fire and swirl the pan lightly till the sugar melts completely. Return to fire on low heat. Wait till sugar caramelizes and turns golden. Add almonds. Pour on a greased kitchen platform. Do not let the sugar turn brown as the caramel turns bitter on doing so. Let caramel cool and then push to remove from surface. Crush caramel with a rolling pin (belan) for the cake.

4. Cut cake into 2 layers.

5. For topping, slice the fruits neatly. Keep about ½ cup chopped fruit to put inside the cake.

6. Place one layer of cake on the serving plate. Soak with 4-5 tbsp orange juice using a silicon brush. Put 2-3 tbsp heaped cream and spread gently.

7. Sprinkle some crushed caramel. Put chopped fruit. Apply crush on the second layer of cake and invert on the fruits. Press. Soak lightly with orange juice.
   6.Cover with cream on the top. Level top with a palette knife dipped in cold water. Cream the sides also. Make a shell border on the edges with the cream in the icing bag, using the small star nozzle. Refrigerate.

8. Decorate with fresh fruits. Stick caramel on the sides.

9. For shine on the fruits, boil sugar and water together in a small pan. Simmer for 5 minutes till it turns syrupy.Add butter and remove from fire. Keep aside to brush on fruits.

10. Brush fruits with the cooled glaze syrup. Refrigerate.

Micky Mousey Cake

Sugar paste icing has opened up a whole new concept to cake decorating. Very easy to use, pliable and can be coloured and moulded and shaped in any form or shape. While making the sugar decorations, keep the rolled out dough and also the total dough always covered with a cling wrap or a thick damp cloth, then put in a well covered box to prevent it from drying. The sugar paste dries up very fast. If the paste becomes dry, keep kneading it till it becomes smooth and pliable.

INGREDIENTS

vanilla cake batter - page 9
¼ cup sugar syrup (boil 2 tbsp sugar with ¼ cup water for 2-3 minutes)

BUTTER ICING
50 gm unsalted butter, softened
100 gm icing sugar - sifted, ½ tsp vanilla essence
1-2 drops lemon food colour

SUGAR PASTE
250 gms icing sugar (2 cups)
1 tsp CMC (carboxy methyl cellulose)
1 tsp glycerine, 1 tsp gelatine, 3 tbsp water

1. Make a cake batter and transfer to a mickey mouse cake mould. Bake in a preheated oven at 160°C/325°F for 30 minutes.

2. For the butter icing, beat together the butter, icing sugar and essence until smooth. Add just a drop of colour and add more if needed.

3. For sugar paste, soak gelatine in 3 tbsp of water for 5 minutes and then melt on low heat or microwave for 15 seconds, to dissolve the gelatine. Sieve the icing sugar and CMC powder together and add glycerine. Add the hot gelatine mixture to it. Knead to a firm and smooth dough. If the consistency of the dough is loose or too soft, add more icing sugar and knead again for 2-3 minutes to get a firm and smooth dough.

4. Leaving a small ball of white fondant for the eyes, divide fondant in 2 parts. To one part, add a drop of yellow colour and a hint of red/pink colour to get skin colour for the face. Add chocolate colour to the other part. Wrap both separately in cling wrap.

5. To decorate the cake, cut cake horizontally and place one part on a tray. Soak with sugar syrup using a silicon brush. Apply butter cream and spread well. Place the other piece of cake on it. Soak with syrup. Cover completely on top and sides with butter cream. Refrigerate for 30 minutes.

6. Roll out skin coloured fondant thinly, using cornflour for dusting, and much bigger than the top of the cake, so as to cover the sides also. Place the rolled fondant on the cake. Press the fondant on the sides of the cake to stick the fondant. Trim off the excess fondant at the bottom with a knife. Level the top with a fondant leveller or the back of a small steel bowl. Add pink colour to the trimmings and make the bow of the Mousey. Make eyes with the white fondant. Roll out the chocolate fondant also. Cut and decorate as shown in the picture.

Black Forest Cake

Serves 16

INGREDIENTS

CHOCOLATE CAKE
½ tin (200 gms) condensed milk
3 tbsp powdered sugar
75 gms butter
100 ml (½ cup) aerated cola drink (pepsi, coke)
3 tbsp cocoa powder
110 gms (1 cup) flour (*maida*)
1 tsp baking powder
½ tsp baking soda (*mitha soda*)

OTHER INGREDIENTS
1 tin of cherries, 1 tbsp rum, optional
100 gms dark chocolate - for the curls

CREAM ICING
200 gms (1 cup) whipping cream
powdered sugar to taste
½ tsp vanilla essence

1. To prepare the chocolate cake, preheat the oven to 150°C/300°F.

2. Mix butter, sugar and condensed milk in a mixing bowl. Beat well.

3. Sift flour, cocoa, baking soda and baking powder together.

4. Add flour gradually to the condensed milk and butter mixture, mixing with a silicon spatula.

5. Add cola and mix well. Immediately transfer to a big square silicon mould. Bake in a preheated oven at 150°C/300°F for 60 minutes or till done. If a knife inserted in the centre of the cake comes out clean, remove from oven. Remove from mould after 5-7 minutes.

6. To make chocolate flakes for decoration, with the help of a vegetable peeler, start peeling the side of the chocolate slab on to a plate, applying a little pressure as you peel. The chocolate should neither be too cold nor too soft. Keep curls in the freezer for half an hour to harden.

7. Grate some chocolate slab from the side on to a plate, to get tiny curls for the sides. Keep the curls spread out in the plate in the freezer.

8. Beat cream till thick. Add sugar and essence and beat carefully till the cream is very thick and can stand in soft peaks. Put some in an icing bag. Keep bag and rest of the cream also in the fridge.

9. Remove seeds from 1 cup cherries. Keep aside. Add rum or essence to 1 cup cherry syrup for soaking.

10. Cut the cake into 3 layers. Place a cake layer on a serving platter. Soak with ¼ cup cherry syrup. Spread some cream. Put deseeded cherries on the cream. Put the second layer of cake. Repeat soaking, spreading cream and cherries.

11. Put the last layer of cake. Soak cake again with ¼ cup syrup. Cover the cake completely with cream on all sides and the top. Level top and sides with a broad knife dipped in chilled water.

12. Make a border on the edge by closely piping swirls of cream from the icing gun. For the lower border, hold the piping bag at such an angle that half the swirl is on the cake and the other half of the swirl is on the platter.

13. Place cherries on swirls. Put big curls on the top. Stick the tiny curls on the sides with a flat spoon.

Cup Cakes

Colourful Cup Cakes

Makes 12

INGREDIENTS

VANILLA CUP CAKES
225 gm flour (*maida*)
1 tsp baking powder
½ tsp baking soda (*mitha soda*)
90 gm butter, softened,
150 gm caster sugar
1¼ cup butter milk (mix 1 cup milk + ¼ cup yogurt), 1 tsp vanilla essence

VANILLA BUTTER CREAM
100 gm unsalted butter, softened
200 gm icing sugar, ½ tsp vanilla essence

CHOCOLATE BUTTER CREAM
100 gm unsalted butter, softened
200 gm icing sugar, ½ tsp vanilla essence
40 gm cocoa powder, or as desired

DECORATION
coloured balls

1. Sift the flour, baking soda and baking powder into a large bowl.

2. Beat butter & caster sugar till fluffy. Add 2 tbsp flour and some butter milk and fold with a spatula till mixed. Add the remaining flour and buttermilk in batches, ending with flour.

3. Spoon mixture into the muffin tray. Bake in the preheated oven at 180°C/350°F for 25 minutes, or until risen, firm and golden brown. .

4. For the butter cream, beat together the butter, icing sugar and vanilla until smooth. For chocolate butter cream, make vanilla icing as above. Mix cocoa powder with 2 tbsp water to make a smooth paste and add to the vanilla icing.

5. Spread or pipe butter cream on top of each cup cake. Decorate with colourful balls.

Note: These cupcakes can be made either in round or heart cupcake moulds provided in the bakeware set. You can also make chocolate cup cakes instead of vanilla as on page 32.

Chocolate Marble Cup Cakes

Makes 12

CHOCOLATE CUP CAKES
190 gms (1¾ cups) flour
180 gms (1½ cups) powdered sugar
4 tbsp cocoa powder
1 tsp baking soda (*mitha soda*)
¼ tsp baking powder, ½ tsp salt
1 cup cold refrigerated water
¼ cup oil
1 tbsp white vinegar, 1 tsp vanilla essence
¼ cup soda water (a bottle of soda)

MARBLE FROSTING
85 gm unsalted butter, softened
150 gm icing sugar - sifted, 1 tsp vanilla essence
½ cup chopped chocolate (60 gm) or 20 gm
cocoa dissolved in 2 tbsp hot water

1. Whisk flour, powdered sugar, cocoa powder, salt, baking powder and baking soda and keep aside.

2. In a big mixing bowl, put cold water, oil, white vinegar and vanilla essence.

3. Add flour, mix in 2-3 batches, folding gently with a silicon spatula each time. Do not over mix.

4. Pour ¼ cup soda water. Mix quickly.

5. Put batter into silicon muffin tray. Bake in preheated oven at 180°C/350°C for 25 minutes or until done. Let cool completely.

6. For the frosting, melt chocolate on a double boiler or make cocoa paste.

7. Beat together the butter, icing sugar and essence until smooth and fluffy. Transfer half of it carefully in a piping bag, spooning it from the side. To the remaining half of the icing add melted chocolate or cocoa paste and mix well. Spoon this chocolate frosting in the same piping bag carefully from the other side of the bag, so as not to mix them.

8. Pipe on cooled cup cakes to get vanilla and chocolate frosting together.

Red Velvet Cup Cakes

Makes 12

150 gms (1⅓ cup) flour (*maida*)
½ tsp baking soda (*mitha soda*)
½ tsp baking powder
¼ tsp salt
1 cup caster sugar
¼ cup butter, room temperature
1 tsp vanilla *essence*
1 tbsp unsweetened cocoa powder, sifted
1 tsp raspberry red food colouring
1 cup buttermilk (¼ cup yogurt + ¾ cup milk)

VANILLA CREAM CHEESE FROSTING
½ cup cream cheese or 1/3 cup cheese spread,
at room temperature
½ cup unsalted butter, room temperature
1 tsp vanilla *essence*
1 cup icing sugar, or to taste

1. Preheat oven at 180°C/350°F.

2. In a medium bowl, whisk together flour, baking soda, baking powder and salt.

3. In a large bowl, beat together butter and sugar until light. Add vanilla *essence*.

4. Add cocoa powder & red food coloring and mix everything on low speed.

5. Gradually add half of the flour mixture and half of the buttermilk. Mix using a silicon spatula. Add remaining flour & buttermilk. Transfer to a silicon muffin tray. Bake for 25 minutes.

6. In a large bowl, beat all ingredients of the frosting, until the icing is smooth and creamy. Check sweetness. Spread or pipe onto cooled cup cakes.

Tiramisu Hearts

Makes 12

INGREDIENTS

CAPPUCCINO CAKE

140 gms (1¼ cups) flour (*maida*)
30 gms (½ cup) cocoa powder
1 tsp baking powder
½ tsp baking soda (*mitha soda*)
¾ cup yogurt
150 gms (1¼ cup) powdered sugar
½ cup oil
3 tsp coffee powder mixed in 1 tbsp hot water
1 tsp vanilla essence
3 tbsp milk

COFFEE SYRUP

2 tsp coffee powder
¼ cup brown sugar, ¾ cup water

ICING

200 gm whipped cream (Rich's cream)
3 tbsp cheese spread or cream cheese
¾ cup icing sugar, or to taste
3 tsp coffee dissolved in 3-4 tbsp water
100 gm milk chocolate

1. For the cake, sift flour, baking powder, soda and cocoa powder together. Combine coffee and hot water. Beat yogurt and sugar to mix well. Add coffee mix and essence. Add oil very gradually, while beating continuously. Fold in sifted flour mixture with a silicon spatula gently. Add 3 tbsp milk. Mix gently. Pour mixture into the heart shape silicon cup cake moulds. Bake in preheated oven at 160°C/325°F for 25-30 minutes.

2. For the coffee syrup, combine sugar and water. Boil and stir over low heat till sugar dissolves. Remove from fire. Add coffee and let it cool.

3. For icing, whip cream till stiff peaks form. Keep aside.

4. Beat cheese spread or cream cheese with sugar in a separate bowl. Mix coffee dissolved in water to the cheese spread. Add whipped cream also with a spatula.

5. Cut the cup cake into 3 layers. Place a cake layer on a serving platter. Brush with coffee syrup. Spread some coffee icing. Put the second layer of cake. Repeat soaking and spreading icing.

6. Put the last layer of cake. Soak cake again. Cover the cup cake completely with cream on top. Put in the fridge.

7. Grate the chocolate bar on a plate and put the plate in the freezer for 10 minutes to harden. Decorate cup cakes with chocolate flakes.

Strawberry Ripple

Makes 12

175 gm (1¾ cups) flour (*maida*)
1½ tsp baking powder
¾ tsp baking soda (*mitha soda*)
60 gm (1 tbsp less than ½ cup) yellow salted butter - softened
100 gm (¾ cup) powdered sugar
½ cup milk
¼ cup strawberry crush or ¼ cup strawberry jam mixed with 1 tbsp water

CREAM CHEESE FROSTING
50 gm unsalted butter
200 gm cream cheese
150 gm icing sugar
a drop of pink colour
½ tsp strawberry essence

1. Sieve the flour, baking powder and baking soda.

2. Beat butter and sugar till light and fluffy.

3. Add half of the flour and half of the milk. Mix well with a silicon spatula and add the remaining milk and flour. Add strawberry crush or jam and mix.

4. Spoon mixture into silicon cup cake moulds, filling them ¾ only.

5. Bake at 180°C/350°F for 20-25 minutes till golden on the top.

6. For the frosting, beat butter till soft. Add cream cheese and beat on low speed for 2 minutes. Gradually add sugar into the bowl and beat for 2-3 minutes till smooth and glossy. Add colour and essence. Check sweetness and add more sugar if required. Refrigerate for 45 minutes or till firm enough to pipe.

7. Pipe frosting on the cooled cup cakes.

Kiwi Cup Cakes with Lemon Frosting

Makes 12

INGREDIENTS

175 gm (1¾ cups) flour (*maida*)
1½ tsp baking powder
¾ tsp baking soda (*mitha soda*)
60 gm (1 tbsp less than ½ cup) yellow salted butter - softened
100 gm (¾ cup powdered sugar)
¼ cup milk
2 kiwi fruit - peeled and chopped finely

FROSTING
55 gm cream cheese, 115 gm icing sugar

1. Sieve the flour, baking powder and baking soda.

2. Beat butter and sugar till light and fluffy.

3. Add half of the flour and half of the milk. Mix well with a silicon spatula and add the remaining milk and flour.

4. Mash kiwi lightly with a fork. Then stir in chopped kiwi fruit in the cup cake batter. Add 1-2 tbsp more milk if required to get a soft dropping consistency.

5. Spoon mixture into silicon cup cake moulds, filling them ¾ only. Bake at 180°C/350°F for 25 minutes till golden on the top. Let the cup cakes cool completely on the wire rack before frosting.

6. For the frosting, beat together the cream cheese and icing sugar until smooth.

7. Pipe or spread the frosting over the cup cakes and top with kiwi fruit slices.

Almond Strawberry Cup Cakes

Makes 12

INGREDIENTS

225 gm flour (*maida*)
2 tbsp flaked almonds or chopped almonds
1 tsp baking powder
½ tsp baking soda (*mitha soda*)
90 gm butter, softened
150 gm caster sugar
1¼ cup butter milk (mix 1 cup milk + ¼ cup yogurt)
1 tsp strawberry essence

STRAWBERRY BUTTER CREAM

100 gm unsalted butter, softened
200 gm icing sugar
½ tsp strawberry essence
a drop of raspberry red colour
a few strawberries - sliced, optional

1. Sift flour, baking soda and baking powder into a large bowl. Add almonds.
2. Beat butter and caster sugar till fluffy and creamy. Add essence.
3. Add 2 tbsp flour and some butter milk and fold with a silicon spatula till mixed. Add the remaining flour and buttermilk in batches, ending with flour.
4. Spoon mixture into the silicon cup cake moulds.
5. Bake at 180°C/350°F in the preheated oven for 25 minutes, or until risen, firm and golden brown.
6. For butter icing, beat butter till smooth. Add the icing sugar gradually and beat until smooth. Add essence and colour.
7. Pipe over the cup cakes and decorate with a fresh strawberry slice.

Muffins

Almond Muffins

Makes 12

INGREDIENTS

150 gms (1¼ cups) powdered sugar
2 cups buttermilk (mix 1½ cup milk and ½ cup yogurt), approx.
90 gms (½ cup) yellow butter
225 gms (2 cups) flour
1 tsp baking powder
½ tsp baking soda (mitha soda)
1 tsp orange essence

SWIRL LATER
¼ cup orange marmalade

TOPPING
3-4 tsp flaked almonds

1. Sift flour, baking powder and baking soda. Keep aside.

2. Beat butter and sugar till soft and fluffy. Add essence and beat again.

3. Add 2 tbsp flour mixture and a little buttermilk. Fold them with a silicon spatula. Add the remaining flour and buttermilk also in batches. Add just enough butter milk to get a soft dropping consistency.

4. Whisk marmalade lightly but do not make it smooth. Fold marmalade into the muffin mix, swirling it just once or twice. Do not mix too much.

5. Pour the mixture in silicon muffin tray, filling them about ¾ full. Top with almond flakes. Press lightly.

6. Bake at 180°C/350°F until done for about 25 minutes. Remove from oven. Let them cool before unmoulding.

Carrot and Banana Muffins

Makes 12

85 gm whole wheat flour (*atta*)
85 gms flour (*maida*)
1½ tsp baking powder
¾ tsp baking soda (*mitha soda*)
1 cup grated carrots
3 tbsp raisins
90 gms (½ cup) yellow salted butter - softened
1 tsp vanilla essence
150 gms (1 cup + 2 tbsp) powdered sugar
2 ripe bananas - chop and then mash with a
fork (1 cup)
1/3 cup milk, approx.

1. Sieve the flours, baking powder and baking soda.

2. Add carrots and raisins to the flour. Keep aside

3. Beat butter, essence and sugar till light and fluffy. Remove the beaters.

4. Add half of the flour and mix well with a silicon spatula. Add the remaining flour and mix to get a thick lumpy batter. Do not over mix. Just mix enough to moisten the dry ingredients.

5. Add mashed bananas and fold to mix. Add just enough milk slowly to get a thick dropping batter.

6. Spoon mixture into a muffin tray, filling cups only ¾ full. Tap lightly. Bake at 180°C/350°F for 25 minutes till golden on the top.

Choco Chip Muffins

Makes 10

190 gms (1¾ cups) flour (*maida*)
½ tsp baking powder
½ tsp baking soda (*mitha soda*)
125 gms (2/3 cup) yellow butter
115 gms (1 cup less 1 tbsp) powdered sugar
1 cup milk, at room temperature
1½ tbsp white vinegar
1 tsp vanilla essence
½ cup chocolate chips

1. Rub flour, baking powder and butter together with the finger tips, till the mixture is crumbly. Do not over mix. Add sugar and mix lightly. Mix chocolate chips and vanilla essence.

2. Divide milk into two parts. To one part which is at room temperature, add vinegar. Warm the other part of milk slightly and add baking soda. Now mix both the milks together.

3. The milk will start foaming (bubbles appear). Add this to the cake mix very quickly. Mix fast and well.

4. Transfer mixture to silicon cup cake moulds. Bake in preheated oven at 190°C/375°F for 10 minutes, then lower the temperature to 150°C/300°F and bake for another 15 minutes.

5. Let the muffins cool for 10 minutes before removing from the moulds. Cool on a wire rack.

Pies & Tarts

Baked Pineapple Roll

Serves 8

INGREDIENTS

WRAP
1 cup flour (*maida*)
½ tsp baking powder
3 tbsp butter - softened

FILLING
1 ripe pineapple - peeled and cut into tiny pieces
2 tbsp sugar, 1 tbsp butter
½ tsp cinnamon (dalchini) powder
1-2 tbsp chopped cashews

SUGAR SYRUP
½ cup sugar
½ cup water
1 tsp butter

6. Roll the remaining flour thinly. Cut into thin strips and arrange over the rolls using a little water.

7. Put the rolls in the big square cake mould and bake in a moderate oven at 160°C/325°F for 1 hour. After 15 minutes prick with a toothpick and brush sugar syrup on the rolls. Again after every 15 minutes, keep brushing the rolls in the same way with sugar syrup.

8. Cut into slices to serve.

1. For the wrap, sift the flour and baking powder together. Rub in 3 tbsp butter with the finger tips. Add just enough ice cold water to bind together. Keep covered in the refrigerator.

2. For the filling, cook pineapple with sugar and butter till dry. Add cinnamon powder. Mix cashews. Keep aside.

3. Boil sugar with water to make the syrup. After the first boil, keep boiling on low heat for about 4-5 minutes. Remove from fire and add 1 tsp butter.

4. Divide the dough into 2 balls. Roll each ball into a rectangle. Cut sides to shape into a neat rectangle.

5. Spread half the pineapple mixture over the dough and roll it like a swiss roll. Prepare the other roll also in the same way.

Lemon Tarts

Makes 10

SHORT CRUST PASTRY

1 cup flour (*maida*)
30 gms butter
6 tsp caster sugar
¼ tsp baking powder
2-3 drops vanilla essence
4-5 tbsp milk, approx.

LEMON FILLING

¾ cup water, ¾ cup sugar, a pinch salt
3½ tbsp cornflour dissolved in 3 tbsp water
1 tsp butter, 2 drops of yellow colour
3 tsp lemon juice, 2 drops of lemon essence
½ cup stiffly whipped cream

DECORATING

a few cherries or strawberries, mint leaves

1. Mix powdered sugar, baking powder and flour. Add butter. Rub with the finger tips till the mixture turns crumbly. Add essence.

2. Make a smooth and semi-firm dough with milk, kneading very lightly. Wrap in a cling wrap & keep in the fridge for 15 minutes.

3. Roll out the pastry 1/8" thin (very thin) between two sheets of plastic. Cut into 4" diameter rounds using a biscuit cutter or a katori or a bottle lid bigger than the round cup cake mould, making sure that they fit the mould well, covering the sides also. Place in the round cup cake mould.

4. Prick with a fork. Cut the edges if you like, to level sides. Bake blind for 15 minutes in the centre of a hot oven at 200°C/400°F till golden in colour on the edges. Take out from oven. Cool.

5. For the lemon jelly, boil water and sugar with a pinch of salt. Simmer on low heat for 5 minutes. Add the cornflour dissolved in water, stirring continuously. Add butter and yellow colour. Cook on medium heat till very thick. Remove from fire and let it cool. Add lemon juice and essence.

6. Spread lemon jelly inside each tart shell, o the bottom and sides.

7. Mix the remaining jelly in stiffly whipped cream to prepare lemon cream icing. Chill in the refrigerator and fill in an icing bag. Pipe into the tart shells to fill nicely. Decorate with fruit and mint.

Fresh Fruit Tarts

Makes 10

SHORT CRUST PASTRY
100 gms (1 cup) flour (*maida*)
6 tsp yellow salted butter - cut into tiny cubes
and chilled
6 tsp powdered sugar
¼ tsp baking powder
a few drops vanilla essence
4-5 tbsp milk to bind

CUSTARD FILLING
3½ tbsp custard powder
1 cup full cream milk, 2 tbsp sugar
2 tbsp thick cream, optional

FRUITS - ALL CUT NEATLY INTO SLICES
1 apple, 1 kiwi, a few strawberries or cherries
few grapes, melon balls
a few mango/papaya slices

OTHER INGREDIENTS
50 gm chocolate - chopped
1 tbsp honey

1. Mix powdered sugar, baking powder and flour. Add butter. Rub with the finger tips till the mixture turns crumbly. Add essence.

2. Make a smooth and semi-firm dough with milk, kneading very lightly. Wrap in a cling wrap & keep in the fridge for 15 minutes.

3. Roll out the pastry 1/8" thin (very thin) between two sheets of plastic. Cut into 4" diameter rounds using a biscuit cutter or a katori or a bottle lid bigger than the round cup cake moulds, making sure that they fit the mould well, covering the sides also. Line with the cut rounds in the moulds. Cut the extra dough if needed. Prick with a fork. Bake blind for 15 minutes in the centre of a hot oven at 200°C/400°F till golden in colour on the edges. Take out from oven. Cool.

4. For the custard, mix custard powder, milk and sugar. Bring to a boil, stirring continuously. Cook for 2-3 minutes more till very thick with a dropping consistency. Let it cool.

5. Soften chocolate in a microwave for 30 seconds. Mix with a brush to melt the chocolate. Spread cooled tart shells with melted chocolate on the bottom and the sides. Fill with thick custard. Top with neatly arranged fruits.

6. Mix 1 tbsp water with honey and brush on the fruits. Serve.

Chocolates

Types of Chocolates

SEMISWEET / DARK CHOCOLATE:

52 to 62% cacao (cacao= cocoa solids + cocoa butter)

Semisweet chocolate is entry level for those who are new to bitter and darker, more pronounced chocolate flavour. This chocolate has a slightly sweet flavour and a dark brown colour. With its accessible flavour and creamy consistency, semisweet chocolate is a dream to work with. It melts easily, combines well with other flavours, and is fantastic for dipping.

semi sweet/dark chocolate

BITTERSWEET:

63 to 72% cacao (cacao = cocoa solids + cocoa butter)

Darker and more pronounced in flavour than a semisweet, bittersweets are the favourites of many chefs. However, their higher cacao content can make them trickier to work with.

MILK CHOCOLATE:

36 to 46% cacao (cacao = cocoa solids + cocoa butter)

As the name suggests, it contains milk solids and has a creamy, mild and sweet flavour. It is light brown in colour and usually not recommended for cooking.

WHITE CHOCOLATE

Since it does not contain cacao solids, white chocolate is technically not a chocolate. Whether or not you're a fan of this bar of cocoa butter, sugar, vanilla, and milk, there are times when it is just right. White chocolate is very sensitive to heat, so be careful when melting it.

white chocolate

UNSWEETENED CHOCOLATE:

100% cacao

Unsweetened chocolate, as the name implies, is 100 percent cacao with no sugar added. One taste will tell you that it is not meant to be eaten alone. I like to use it in combination with semi or bittersweet to add depth of flavour.

COCOA POWDER

Cocoa is the pure chocolate mass which is left when the cocoa butter has been removed from the chocolate liquor. It is then ground and sifted. Cocoa lends desserts and baked goods, a wonderful depth of flavour.

cocoa powder

Storing Chocolate

Chocolate should be kept in its wrapper in a box and stored in a cool, dry dark place, away from direct sunlight or heat. If storing an opened bar, wrap in its paper and then in a sealed plastic bag. The best storage temperature is 62 to 70° F. I do not recommend refrigeration because the condensation that occurs can result in sugar bloom (or grains on the surface). If you live in a hot place without air conditioning, however, there may be no option. So, chocolate can be refrigerated in summer, but it is necessary to bring it to room temperature before chopping or grating. Chocolate melts in the low nineties - a pleasure when it's in your mouth and a potential disaster in a very hot kitchen.

The whitish colour that can rise to the top on chocolate is called fat bloom. It means the cocoa butter has separated and risen to the top due to heat. As unappealing as it looks, the final taste is not affected, because when the chocolate is melted, the cocoa butter will be redistributed throughout the chocolate.

Chopping Chocolate

To chop chocolate, the best tool is a long serrated knife and a heavy wooden board. Starting on a corner of a block or square of chocolate, cut ¼" thick slices along the diagonal, pressing both the hands on either side of the knife. The chocolate will naturally break into thin chips as you cut. Keep turning the chocolate square to work evenly off all the corners.

Special Essences

Moisture is a great enemy of chocolate. Even a drop of water can ruin the melted chocolate. Hence the choice of essence should be made carefully. Special oil bound essences are available for adding to the chocolate. The regular essences are water based and hence cannot be added to pure chocolate. However, these water based essences can be used in the centre fillings which are made with cream and icing sugar or in truffles where chocolate is mixed with cream to make the centre filling.

Melting Chocolate in a Double Boiler

Chocolate is very sensitive to heat and moisture. Once you learn the art of melting chocolate, working with it becomes very simple. Prevent any water or steam coming into contact with the melted chocolate. A small amount of liquid, even a wet spoon or steam may cause the chocolate to seize and stiffen, making it unusable.

1. The chocolate slab should be at room temperature at the time of melting. Cut chocolate into thin pieces.

2. Put chocolate in a stainless steel bowl that can fit well over a sauce pan, without having space on the sides for the steam to escape. This makes a good double boiler. If steam goes into the melting chocolate, it may ruin the chocolate. Fill saucepan with 1" water and put it on fire to boil. When water boils, reduce heat to minimum.

3. Place the bowl of chocolate on the simmering water, making sure that the base of the bowl does not come into contact with water and the heat is very low. The water should not be boiling rapidly. Do not stir. Once the chocolate starts to melt, very gently stir with a silicon spatula or a spoon. When almost melted, switch off the fire.

4. Remove bowl from saucepan and place on a towel placed on the kitchen platform. This absorbs the moisture at the base of the bowl. Gently stir again for 2-3 minutes with the silicon spatula till fully melted, smooth and glossy.

Note: Do not melt chocolate over direct heat (unless melting with other ingredients - in this case keep the heat very low).

Melting Chocolate in a Microwave

This can be quite tricky at times. Melt very gradually, increasing the time only after checking the chocolate. Never melt the chocolate fully, once it softens it melts by itself on simply stirring it with a silicon spatula.

1. Cut the chocolate into small pieces. Place in a microwave-proof bowl.

2. Put the bowl in the microwave oven and melt. As a guide, melt 125 gm dark chocolate on high power for 1 minute and white or milk chocolate on medium power for 2-3 minutes.

3. Stir the chocolate with a silicon spatula, let stand for a few minutes, then stir again if necessary. Return to the microwave for another 30 seconds if required.

Tips to make Perfect Chocolates

1. Usually the dark variety is used. Milk chocolates are good for children. Generally 100 gm chocolate when chopped is equal to about 1 cup.

2. Wipe chocolate trays with a muslin cloth. Even a drop of moisture in the tray will turn melted chocolate into a solid mass. Such chocolates cannot be used. When in a rush, using a hair dryer to dry the chocolate trays is a good idea.

3. Prepare a good double boiler for melting chocolate. See that no steam escapes from the sides of the bowl. Steam gives moisture to chocolate, turning it useless.

4. While melting chocolate, too much heat burns the chocolate. It loses it's lustre and shine. Keep the heat very low and put off the flame as soon as the chocolate softens. Sitting on the double boiler on hot water will melt the chocolate completely.

5. The prepared chocolates should preferably be set in the fridge and not in the freezer. The freezer has moisture in it.

6. When you fill the melted chocolate in the tray, quickly invert the mould and tap each mould just once to take out the excess. Do not tap too much, or you will not get a nice shell. Keep in the freezer for about 10 minutes to set.

7. To make centres with cream, use tetra packs of cream as they are stabilized and stay good for a long time. Fresh cream from the dairy should be avoided. Never heat the cream too much and never add chocolate to very hot cream. The fat separates on doing so. Remove the cream from heat and wait for a few seconds before you add the chocolate.

8. Let the filling come to room temperature before you put it in the chocolate shells. If you put hot filling you might end up having a chocolate with a hole.

9. When you put the centre in the shell for moulded chocolate, do not put too much of centre filling as it might come out of the chocolate covering. About ¼-½ tsp is enough in each shell. Leave enough space for the top layer of chocolate covering. Now keep in the fridge or freezer to set.

10. Before you put the final layer of melted chocolate, check that the filling is set.

Basic Steps to Make Moulded Chocolates

Chocolates can be made into different shapes using a chocolate tray. A variety of fillings can be used to fill chocolates. The recipe of various fillings for the centre of chocolates follow later. Here we give you the basic way for making all chocolates with centre fillings. The variety of centre fillings follow later.

Makes 1 chocolate tray

150 gm dark chocolate - cut into small pieces

1. Prepare the centre filling. Keep filling aside. Melt covering chocolate in a double boiler as given on page 50. Remove from hot water on a kitchen towel spread on the kitchen platform to absorb any moisture at the bottom of the bowl. Keep stirring with a silicon spatula for 2-3 minutes to temper the chocolate and bring it to room temperature. The chocolate will turn very smooth and glossy. Do not fill hot chocolate into the tray.

2. Spoon melted chocolate in chocolate tray to fill the moulds fully. Tap on the kitchen surface 1-2 times.

3. Invert the tray, holding the tray over the cleaned kitchen platform for the extra chocolate to come out and the chocolate left just coats the mould. If you like, tap 1-2 times with a palette knife to remove the extra chocolate to make thin shells.

4. Invert to get the right side up. Level chocolate with a palette knife, dropping the excess chocolate on the kitchen slab. Keep tray in the freezer for 10 minutes.

5. Take out the set chocolate tray. Spoon ¼ - ½ tsp of filling mixture in each shell, pushing the filling into the shell with the help of a table knife, if need be. Keep in the fridge to set for 10-15 minutes. Do not fill too much, keep ¼ of the shell empty.

6. When the filling feels slightly set when touched with a finger, spoon melted chocolate over the filling to cover the filling completely.

7. Spoon chocolate generously it till it comes out a little from the sides. This over filling of the covering chocolate seals the filling nicely. Shake the tray lightly to level. Do not tap the tray.

8. Scrape off the excess chocolate gently with a palette knife. Run the knife once forwards. Keep tray in the fridge to set for at least 2 hours.

9. Invert the tray and tap lightly to unmould the chocolates.

10. Neaten the edges of the chocolate using a knife. Store covered and refrigerated.

11. Scrape the chocolate on the kitchen platform with a chocolate scraper. This chocolate can be melted again and reused.

Caramel Chocolates

Makes one tray

INGREDIENTS

CENTRE FILLING
4 tbsp sugar
4 tbsp thin cream (to be at room temp)
1 tbsp water at room temp.

COVERING CHOCOLATE
150 gm dark cooking chocolate - cut into small pieces

1. To prepare the centre, measure cream and keep ready in a small bowl. Spread the sugar in a small flat pan. Keep on medium heat, without touching or stirring for about 1-2 minutes. When the sides turn light golden, lift the pan off the fire and rotate the pan gently to evenly brown the sugar. Return to fire on low heat for 1-2 minutes. When sugar melts properly and it turns a rich golden, remove from fire. Add cream and mix well with a silicon spatula till smooth. Add 1 tbsp water. Mix well. Cook caramel for 5-7 seconds to get a smooth consistency. Remove from fire. Remove caramel from pan to a bowl immediately to avoid over cooking it on the hot pan. Keep aside.

2. After preparing the filling, follow steps on page 52 to make the chocolates.

Strawberry Chocolate

Makes one tray

CENTRE

6 tbsp sifted icing sugar
4 tbsp thick cream
1 tsp cornflour
½ tsp strawberry essence
a drop of pink or red colour

COVERING CHOCOLATE

150 gms dark cooking chocolate - cut into small pieces

1. To prepare the centre, mix cream, icing sugar and cornflour in a small heavy bottomed pan or kadhai. Cook on low heat stirring continuously for 3-4 minutes with silicon spatula till it becomes slightly thick and the raw taste of cornflour disappears. Add essence and colour. Keep aside till the chocolate shells are set.

2. Melt covering chocolate in a double boiler. Remove from hot water on a kitchen towel spread on the kitchen platform to absorb any moisture at the bottom of the bowl. Keep stirring with a rubber spatula for 2-3 minutes to temper the chocolate and bring it to room temperature. Do not fill hot chocolate into the tray.

3. Spoon melted chocolate in a chocolate tray to fill the moulds nicely. Tap 1-2 times.

4. Invert the tray and holding the tray over the cleaned kitchen platform, tap 1-2 times with a palette knife to remove the extra chocolate and make shells. Invert to get the right side up. Scrape off the excess chocolate with a palette knife. Keep tray in the freezer for 10 minutes.

5. Take out the set chocolate tray. Spoon ¼ - ½ tsp of filling mixture in each shell, pushing the filling into the shell with the help of a table knife. Keep in the fridge to set. (Do not fill too much.)

6. When the filling is slightly set, spoon melted chocolate to cover the top. Spoon chocolate generously till it comes out a little from the sides. This seals the filling.

7. Scrape off the excess chocolate gently with a palette knife. Keep the tray in the fridge to set for at least 2 hours. Invert the tray and tap lightly to unmould the chocolates. Store covered and refrigerated.

Coconut Almond Chocolates

Makes one tray

INGREDIENTS

CENTRE FILLING
4 tbsp desiccated coconut
2 tsp powdered sugar
15 almonds - blanced
peeled and finely chopped

COVERING CHOCOLATE
150 gm dark cooking chocolate - cut into
small pieces

1. To prepare the centre, grind almonds to a rough paste, using 1-2 tsp water.

2. Mix coconut and sugar in the almond paste. Check sweetness.

3. Melt covering chocolate in a double boiler. Remove from hot water on a kitchen towel spread on the kitchen platform to absorb any moisture at the bottom of the bowl. Keep stirring with a silicon spatula for 2-3 minutes to temper the chocolate and bring it to room temperature. Do not fill hot chocolate into the tray.

4. Spoon melted chocolate in chocolate tray to fill the moulds nicely. Tap 1-2 times.

5. Invert the tray and holding the tray over the cleaned kitchen platform, tap 1-2 times with a palette knife to remove the extra chocolate and make shells.

6. Invert to get the right side up. Scrape off the excess chocolate with a palette knife. Keep tray in the freezer for 10 minutes. Keep the remaining chocolate on hot water in the double boiler.

7. Take out the set chocolate tray. Spoon ¼ - ½ tsp of filling mixture in each shell, pushing the filling into the shell with the help of a table knife. Keep in the fridge to set. (Do not fill too much.)

8. When the filling is slightly set, spoon melted chocolate to cover the top. Spoon chocolate generously till it comes out a little from the sides. This seals the filling.

9. Scrape off the excess chocolate gently with a palette knife. Keep the tray in the fridge to set for at least 2 hours. Invert the tray and tap lightly to unmould the chocolates. Store covered and refrigerated.

10. Melt the remaining chocolate on a double boiler and reuse.

Note: Desiccated coconut should be stored in the fridge as the oil in it turns rancid.

Crispy Chocolates

Makes one tray

INGREDIENTS

150 gms cooking chocolate - chopped
2-3 tbsp almonds - chopped
3 tbsp raisins (*kishmish*)
4 tbsp wheat flakes

1. Roast almonds in a pan on very low heat, stirring continuously, till fragrant. Add raisins and roast for another 2 minutes on low heat. Remove from pan as soon as the almonds start to change colour.

2. Melt the chocolate on a double boiler as given on page 50. Remove chocolate from heat. Stir till it comes to room temperature.

3. Stir in the almonds and raisins. Keep aside for a few minutes till it starts to become slightly thick. It should not be too runny, nor should you let it turn too thick.

4. Add wheat flakes to the thickened chocolate.

5. With a spoon, drop rough heaps of the chocolate mixture onto a plate lined with aluminium foil.

6. Leave in the fridge to set for atleast 1-2 hours. Wrap in decorative paper Serve.

Sticky Centre Chocolates

Makes 2 tray

INGREDIENTS

CENTRE
3 tbsp liquid glucose
3 tbsp sugar syrup of one string consistency
see in the method
½ -1 tsp orange or strawberry essence or any
flavour of your choice
a pinch of colour

COVERING CHOCOLATE
250 gm dark cooking chocolate - cut into
small pieces

1. To prepare the syrup, boil ¼ cup sugar and ¼ cup water. Keep on medium flame for about 5 minutes till a one string consistency is ready. The syrup feels sticky when pulled between the thumb and the forefinger. Keep aside.

2. Mix 3 tbsp liquid glucose with 2 tbsp of the above syrup. Add essence and colour. Keep in the fridge to become slightly thick as it cools down.

3. After preparing the filling, follow steps on page 52 to make the chocolates

Chocolate Truffle

Makes 30-35

INGREDIENTS

TRUFLE CENTRE

250 gms dark chocolate - cut into small pieces
100 gm (½ cup) cream, (any tetra pack cream)
1½ - 2 tbsp of rum or 1 tsp rum essence,
optional
1 tbsp icing sugar to coat

COVERING

250 gm dark chocolate - chopped
50 gm white chocolate - chopped (½ cup) for
making lines

1. For the truffle centre, warm cream in a heavy bottomed saucepan, on low heat. Do not boil. Add chopped chocolate. Cook on very low heat stirring continuously for about 5 minutes, till the sauce thickens and starts leaving the sides. Remove from fire. Wait for a minute. Add rum. Mix well. Transfer to a small bowl. When you remove the mixture from fire it is thin but it firms up on keeping.

2. Put truffle mixture in the freezer for at least ½-1 hour or till firm enough to make round balls. Make balls. Roll in icing sugar to coat. Place on a plate lined with aluminium foil. Keep in the fridge.

3. Once the balls are set, melt the chocolate for covering as given on page 50. Remove the melted chocolate from the hot water and stir with a silicon spatula for 2 minutes till it becomes glossy & cools down to room temperature.

4. Add 3-4 balls to the melted chocolate. Stir with a fork to coat chocolate. Remove balls from the melted chocolate. Shake off the excess. Place chocolate coated balls on the foil.

5. To make lines on the ball, make a tight paper cone and secure with scotch tape. Melt white chocolate in the microwave for 30 seconds till soft. Mix well to make a smooth paste. Put melted chocolate in a paper cone. Pipe lines on the chocolate balls. Refrigerate for 3-4 hours.

Mint Chocolates

Makes one tray

150 gm dark cooking chocolate - cut into pieces
½ tsp peppermint essence, oil based

1. Melt covering chocolate in a double boiler as given on page 50. Remove from hot water on a kitchen towel spread on the kitchen platform to absorb any moisture at the bottom of the bowl. Keep stirring with a rubber spatula for 2-3 minutes to temper the chocolate and bring it to room temperature. Add essence and mix well. Do not fill hot chocolate into the tray.

2. Spoon melted chocolate in chocolate tray to fill the moulds nicely. Tap 1-2 times. Scrape off the excess chocolate gently with a palette knife.

3. Keep the tray in the fridge to set for at least 2 hours. Invert the tray and tap lightly to unmould the chocolates. Store covered and refrigerated.

Paan Chocolates

Makes one tray

INGREDIENTS

150 gm dark cooking chocolate - cut into pieces
½ tsp paan essence, oil based

1. Melt covering chocolate in a double boiler as given on page 50. Remove from hot water on a kitchen towel spread on the kitchen platform to absorb any moisture at the bottom of the bowl. Keep stirring with a rubber spatula for 2-3 minutes to temper the chocolate and bring it to room temperature. Add essence and mix well. Do not fill hot chocolate into the tray.

2. Spoon melted chocolate in chocolate tray to fill the moulds nicely. Tap 1-2 times. Scrape off the excess chocolate gently with a palette knife.

3. Keep the tray in the fridge to set for at least 2 hours. Invert the tray and tap lightly to unmould the chocolates. Store covered and refrigerated.

Savoury Delights

Macaroni Cheese

Serves 3-4

INGREDIENTS

1 cup macaroni - boiled
1 tsp olive oil
2 tbsp butter
½ small onion - very finely chopped
2 tbsp flour (*maida*)
1½ cups milk
½ tsp salt, ½ tsp pepper
1 tsp tomato ketchup
25 gm cheese - grated
2 tbsp dry bread crumbs
¼ cup frozen corn

1. Melt butter in a small saucepan over medium heat.

2. Add onions and saute for 2 minutes.

3. Add flour, and stir continuously for 30 seconds. Remove from fire.

4. Add milk, stirring continuously. Return to fire. Cook until smooth and slightly thickened such that it coats the spoon, stirring constantly.

5. Add corn, salt and pepper powder. Remove from heat.

6. Add macaroni. Stir in the grated cheese until melted. Add ketchup.

7. Transfer to a big square silicon mould. Sprinkle dry bread crumbs on top. Bake in a hot oven at 180°C/350°F for 10-15 minutes. Serve hot.

Onion Focaccia

Makes 2

INGREDIENTS

DOUGH
2 cups plain flour (*maida*)
2 tsp dry yeast, 1 tsp sugar
1 tsp oregano, ¾ tsp salt
1½ tsp crushed garlic
½ tsp green chilli paste
2 tbsp olive oil

TO BE MIXED INTO A TOPPING
1 tsp oregano
1 small onion - finely chopped
1 tsp chilli flakes
2 tsp olive oil, ½ tsp salt

OTHER INGREDIENTS FOR TOPPING
1 small red capsicum - cut into ½" squares
a few sliced black olives

1. In a deep bowl, put ½ cup warm water and 1 tsp sugar. Mix and sprinkle the dry yeast over it. Cover the bowl and leave in a closed warm place for 10-15 minutes till frothy.

2. Combine flour, oregano, salt, garlic, chilli paste. Add the yeast mixture and mix well. Knead with enough warm water to a very smooth, soft and elastic-dough.

3. Add the olive oil and knead again till very smooth. Grease a large bowl. Put the dough in and turn all over to coat it with oil. See that the bowl is big enough, having enough space for the dough to rise.

4. Cover the bowl with a wrap and allow it to prove for 1½-2 hours, or till it doubles in volume.

5. Punch the dough lightly to remove the air. Divide into 2 balls.

6. Roll out a ball into a square or circle of about ¾" thickness.

7. Place the dough on a greased big square silicon mould and spread the topping mixture onto it. Arrange capsicums and olives on it. Keep aside to prove for 30 minutes. It will double in volume again.

8. Bake in a pre-heated oven at 210°C/430°F for 20-25 minutes or until the focaccia is golden brown. Remove from the oven and brush with olive oil. Serve.

Baked Lasagna

Serves 6-8

INGREDIENTS

4 lasagna sheets
1 cup grated cheddar cheese
1 cup grated mozzarella cheese

RED VEGETABLE SAUCE

4 tbsp olive oil, 4 large tomatoes
8-10 flakes garlic - crushed
1 onion - chopped
1 small carrot - cut into small pieces
1 long brinjal (*baigan*) - peeled cut into small
pieces or 8-10 french beans, chopped
1 small zucchini - cut into small pieces
¼ cup corn kernels
¼ cup tomato puree, 1 tbsp hot and sweet chilli
sauce or tomato ketchup
1 tsp salt, 1 tsp oregano, 1 tsp red chilli flakes

WHITE SAUCE

3 tbsp butter, 3 tbsp flour (*maida*)
2½ cups milk
¾ tsp salt, ¼ tsp pepper

1. Boil whole tomatoes in water for 3-4 minutes. Cool, peel and blend tomatoes to a smooth puree.

2. Heat olive oil in a pan, add garlic and saute slightly. Add onion and cook till soft and transparent. Add the pureed tomatoes to the onion and stir for a minute. Add the chopped vegetables - carrots, brinjal/beans and zucchini. Mix and add ½ cup water. Cook till the vegetables are soft.

3. Add corn. Stir and add tomato puree, tomato ketchup, salt, oregano and chilli flakes. Cook on low heat till the sauce gets a slightly thick coating consistency. Remove from heat.

4. For the white sauce, melt butter, add flour and stir for a minute. Remove from heat and add milk slowly, stirring constantly with the other hand. Return to heat and cook till you get a sauce of a thin coating consistency.

5. To assemble, in a big square silicon mould, put 1/3 of the red vegetable sauce. Wet the lasagna sheets under running water. Arrange lasagna sheets over the sauce.

6. Spread 1/3 of the white sauce over the sheet. Sprinkle both the cheese over the white sauce. Put some red vegetable sauce, then wet another sheet and place on the red sauce. Spread some white sauce and then both the cheese on top. Repeat the red sauce, sheets, white sauce and top with cheese.

7. Cover the dish with foil and bake at 180°C /350°F for 35 minutes. Remove foil and bake uncovered for 10 minutes to brown the cheese. Serve.